I0176783

The Power of
Resilience

CORNERSTON
U B L I S H I N

VICTORIA SHOWUNMI

The Power of Resilience
Copyright © 2017 by **Victoria Showunmi**

ISBN: 978-1-952098-12-3

This publication may not be reproduced, stored in a retrieval system, or transmitted in whole or in part, in any form or by any means, electronic, mechanical, photocopying, recording, or otherwise, without the prior written permission of the publisher.
All rights reserved.

Unless otherwise noted, all Scripture quotations are from the King James Version of the Bible. Copyright ©1993, 1996 by Thomas Nelson, Inc. Used by permission. All rights reserved.

Printed in United States of America

Cornerstone Publishing
A Division Cornerstone Creativity Group LLC
Phone: +1(516) 547-4999
info@thecornerstonepublishers.com
www.thecornerstonepublishers.com

To order this book or for speaking engagement:
Victoria Showunmi
www.victoriashowunmi.com
victoria@victoriashowunmi.com
+1 631.741.0795
Facebook.com/womenef
Instagram.com/vickieshow4u
Twitter.com/vickieshow4u

Praise For The Power of Resilience

"In this book, Pastor Victoria highlighted the truth that failure is never the end, but rather a pedestal for upward and onward accomplishment through the power of Resilence. I fully recommend this book for everyone that desire to attain great heights in life."

—Benjamin Beckley
Empowerment Center
Arlington TX

"There is no success without struggle. Victoria had done a huge service to all seeking success. She has boiled down the numerous secrets of success to the one undisputed recipe for success. Master this and you need nothing else. A must read for all."

—Victor Lofinmakin
Top Producing Agent
KW Commercial
Houston, TX

"Ms. Showunmi's story is inspiring and uplifting. Through faith, believing in yourself and embracing the power of positive thinking, one can achieve life goals. The message to live your dream and ultimately achieve your goals through desire, determination and resiliency can be palpated throughout the book. You will enjoy the ride!"

—Donna Ukanowicz
Director, UT MD Anderson Cancer Center,
Houston, TX

"This book will inspire you to take action and not give up."

—Abiola Saba
Mentor, Speaker and Trainer,
New Jersey

"Having known Pastor Victoria for more than a decade, everything in this book is the reason she is one of the most resilient women I know. This book will challenge you to do more, achieve more, never quit on yourself, and step into greatness. It's a great read!"

—Gbenga Showunmi
Senior Pastor,
Destinystar Ministries International

CONTENTS

DEDICATION

To my wonderful husband, Pastor Gbenga Showunmi, and my destiny children – Toluwani, Oluwatobi and Temitayo Showunmi. Words are not enough to express the joy and fulfillment you bring into my life. Each day I thank God for your lives for making me part of it and to experience the joy of a wife and mother. You are such a blessing.

ACKNOWLEDGMENTS

My profound gratitude goes to the Almighty God, who is my strength, my source, and my maker. Without Him, this book wouldn't have been possible. To my husband, my rock, my motivator, my encourager, words cannot express how grateful I am for all your support. The Lord will continue to increase you on every side. To all my family members, mentors, friends and fans, thank you so much.

To the Cornerstone Publishing team, you are such a wonderful team of experts. Thanks for making this book a reality. I pray for more grace and strength upon your lives and ministry.

And to all who will read this book, thank you for believing in me. May the Lord perfect everything that concerns you. I look forward to hearing your testimonies. You are blessed!

INTRODUCTION

D o you sometimes ask yourself, "How long can I keep going, with all the challenges I have to deal with?" Or do you sometimes feel you do not have the strength, enthusiasm, motivation and willpower to move forward? We all do, but what ultimately differentiates the winners from the losers in the journey of life is their ability to hang on to their vision and mission, regardless of the storms and turbulences that threaten to overpower them.

This is one of the major secrets you will discover in this book. It is divinely inspired to re-energize your faith, re-awaken your purpose and reinforce your entire being with renewed strength and grace to keep moving forward till your destiny is fulfilled.

Nothing is over until it is over. Your case is not closed until God intervenes. If God has not given up on you, why should you? If God has not called you home to be with Him, why should you consider yourself finished? That you are still alive to come across a book like this is an indication that God is still very much interested in your life and destiny. It is a sign that you are still expected to fulfill your purpose and vision in life.

Jesus Christ, in John 16:33, says, "These things I have spoken to you, that in Me you may have peace. In the world you will have tribulation; but be of good cheer, I have overcome the world." What this means is that as long as you are on earth, you must continue to fight and win every battle that comes your way; you have to continue to pursue until you realize your dreams; you have to continue to dream big, until your God-ordained destiny is fully filled.

Regardless of how bad things may seem for you currently, giving up is not an option. As it was in the case of Lazarus in the Bible who had been dead for four days and all hopes had seemed lost until Christ intervened, your case is not closed. Your situation is not too difficult for God to handle. If you can believe, He will turn your misery into a miracle.

No matter what you have heard, no matter the negativity about your life and destiny, reading this book will open your inner eyes and enlighten your understanding so that you can persist and pursue until you overtake and recover all your losses.

Success does not come without a price. Without a test, there can be no testimony; without a fight, there can be no victory; without challenges and obstacles to overcome, there can be no success and breakthrough. If it was easy to become an achiever without going through tough times, there shouldn't be failures in life. It is resilience that separates champions from quitters. God has given us all things that we need to excel in life, but we have to choose to either fight for what we want, press through every obstacle and come out as a champions; or to succumb to challenges, live life as a mediocre and eventually exit the world without any sign that we were ever here.

Remember, greatness is on the other side of comfort. This book will give you reasons to continue to persist, to continue to press for that which will differentiate you and position you for greatness in life. As you digest and apply the messages in it, the grace, strength and courage you need to reach your goal and live an impactful life will be released upon you.

Get set for transforming revelations that will exceed your imaginations!

CHAPTER 1

WHO SAYS YOU'RE A FAILURE?

1

WHO SAYS YOU'RE A FAILURE?

"If you are really going to do something in life, the secret is learning how to lose. Nobody goes undefeated all the time. If you can pick up after a crushing defeat, and go on to win again, you are going to be a champion someday."

—Wilma Rudolph

When Wilma Rudolph made history in 1960 as the first American woman to win three gold medals in one Olympics, millions of people rejoiced with her and acknowledged that she was, indeed, an extraordinary sprinter. What many did not know, however, was that this same world champion had participated during the previous Olympics but had gone uncelebrated because she only managed to win a bronze medal. Nor would they know that if human predictions and expectations were anything to go by,

Wilma shouldn't have even been able to walk properly, much less become a record-breaking runner.

Wilma had been born prematurely; thus her early life had been a rollercoaster of illnesses and infections, including pneumonia and scarlet fever. Then came the worst of all – polio, which left her left leg crooked and her foot twisted inward. Her family doctors, after examining her, dropped the bombshell: Wilma would never be able to walk again. She had to start wearing metal leg braces.

Fortunately, after seven years of painful therapy, Wilma soon began to walk without her braces. At age 12, she tried to join a girls' basketball team, but didn't make it. Undaunted, she practiced with a girlfriend and two boys every day. The next year she made the team. When a college track coach saw her during a game, he convinced her to let him train her as a runner. By age 14 Wilma had become one of the fastest sprinters in the U.S.

Following what was considered her mediocre performance at the 1956 Olympics in Melbourne, Australia, Wilma refused to be discouraged; instead she resolved to prove to the world that she could be number one. According to her, "I ran and ran and ran every day, and I acquired this sense of determination, this sense of spirit that I would never, never give up, no matter what else happened."

Then came the 1960 Olympics, and the world was astonished to watch Wilma achieve what no other woman in history had accomplished.

Failure is Not Final

The rest, as they say, is history. But one thing that resonates throughout the story of Wilma's rise to the top is that failure in any area of life is not final. It is not the end of your life. Even if circumstances or people around you try to make you feel hopeless and worthless because of the mistakes you have made or the number of times you have failed, it does not reflect the exact picture of your true destiny. In fact, that you tried and failed is an indication that you are a potential candidate for success. As someone once said, "A life spent making mistakes is not only more honorable but more useful than a life spent in doing nothing."

It may interest you to know that, just like Wilma Rudolph, most of the successful people we hear or read about today in all fields of human endeavor are people who have faced humiliating difficulties, failures and disappointments in life. They have been faced with ridicule, reproach, mockery, and rejection. But rather than allow such setbacks to destroy their enthusiasm or self-esteem, they chose to learn valuable lessons that enabled them to do better with subsequent attempts, until their moments of breakthrough came.

I once read the story of Oprah Winfrey's rise to fame. When she applied to be a newscaster at one TV station, she was turned down because she wasn't considered good enough. She did not let that stop her. Oprah continued to strive for the best while working for her big break to arrive. Once it happened, she was on a continuous run for about 25 years and attracted a massive global audience. Now she has moved on to owning her own TV station and providing a platform of success for other people. Can you imagine that!

But there are even more examples. Many people know Michael Jordan to be one of the greatest basketball players of all time. Looking at the dazzling record of his sterling achievements, one would think it's all because he was too brilliant to have failed. But here's what he had to say about himself: "I've missed more than 9000 shots in my career. I've lost almost 300 games. Twenty-six times I've been trusted to take the game winning shot and missed. I've failed over and over and over again in my life. And that is why I succeed."

George Bernard Shaw, one of the greatest literary writers of the 20th century said, "When I was young,

I observed that nine out of ten things I did were failures. So I did ten times more work.".

What of J.K. Rowling, the brain behind the popular Harry Potter series? She said, "It is impossible to live without failing at something, unless you live so cautiously that you might as well not have lived at all, in which case you have failed by default."

Failure Doesn't Define You

Past failures do not mean that you don't have a greater future ahead of you. The fact that people have criticized, condemned, berated or disappointed you doesn't mean that you are a never-do-well. The fact that you have been turned you down for a position or an opportunity doesn't mean that God does not have a brighter future for you. These are experiences that will make your story unique and interesting when your success and greatness emerge.

Many people today know Theodor Seuss Geisel (Dr. Seuss) as a great cartoonist, animator and best-selling author of several of the most popular children's books of all time. By the time of his death in 1991, over 500 million copies of his books had been sold, many of which had been translated into numerous languages of the world. Yet, nothing about the beginning of his career as a writer gave any hint that he was ever going to be so successful. He faced a lot of frustration and rejection but he persisted and his persistence eventually paid off. To use his exact words: "When I first started writing, I had a lot of struggles. My first book, "And To Think it Happened on Mulberry Street" was rejected 27 times before it finally got published."

Dr. Seuss was not alone. In 1905, the University of Bern turned down a scientific dissertation from a budding researcher and described it as "irrelevant and fanciful." That researcher was Albert Einstein. And, of course, I do not need to bore you here with already known details of how he went on to become one of the greatest scientists in history. Earlier, in 1894, an English teacher had noted on a teenager's report card that he demonstrated "a conspicuous lack of success." In fact, his father had been so frustrated by his repeated underperformance at school that he once said to him, "If you cannot prevent yourself from leading the idle, useless, unprofitable life you have had during your school days…you will become a…social wastrel." That student was Sir Winston Churchill. He went on to become the Prime Minister of Britain!

Failure Refines for Excellence

Henry Ford was right when he said, "The only real mistake is the one from which we learn nothing."

There is a reason we make mistakes and encounter failure in our lives. It is for us to learn something new – something that will bring us closer to the fulfillment of our dreams.

So, failure is not necessarily synonymous with incompetence or incapability. It doesn't mean that you are dumb or daft. It only means that you have been able to identify one way of doing things that will not lead you to your expected result.

Failure is a way of learning. It is a catalyst of growth. In fact, here is one paradox about failure that should always ring in your mind. Failure is often the easiest doorway to success. Put simply, most of the biggest successes, breakthroughs, innovations and triumphs ever recorded in history would not have happened without previous failures.

Take the case of Thomas Edison, for instance. Someone once said of him: "If he hadn't failed, Thomas Edison might not have become America's most well-known and prolific innovator." And, as if to confirm this himself, Thomas Edison, in the January 1921 issue of The American Magazine, recalled an experience he had with one of his colleagues in the laboratory: "After we had conducted thousands of experiments on a certain project without solving the problem, one of my associates, after we had conducted the crowning experiment and it had proved a failure, expressed discouragement and disgust over our having failed to find out anything. I cheerily assured him that we had learned something. For we had learned for a certainty that the thing couldn't be done that way, and that we would have to try some other way."

That was the declaration of one who clearly understood the benefit in failure and went ahead to record great accomplishments in life. Let this apply to you, too, whenever you seem to be hitting a brick wall in achieving a target. Take some time out to think and evaluate. Why did you fail? Were there vital issues that you overlooked? Were there important steps that you ignored? Did you fail because you did not make sufficient preparation? Did you fail because you lacked some essential information? Did you fail because you did not gather all the resources and knowledge needed? In other words, could things have been done differently?

The point is that each time you miss the mark, each time you don't seem to get it right, it's not the end; it's a matter of re-evaluating and launching out again. Do not let negativity overpower your thinking. You don't give up just because you don't get it the first time, or the second time, or even the third time. You try again and again in other legitimate ways. You devise other means and methods until you achieve the results you want.

CHAPTER 2

THE SUCCESS
MENTALITY

2

THE SUCCESS MENTALITY

"I will persist until I succeed. Always will I take another step. If that is of no avail I will take another, and yet another. In truth, one step at a time is not too difficult. I know that small attempts, repeated, will complete any undertaking."

—Og Mandino

One major factor that determines whether failure will confine or refine you is your perception of success – do you consider it negotiable or non-negotiable? Everyone in life experiences failure at one time or the other. However, what ultimately distinguishes winners from losers in their confrontations with failure is the quality of their thinking. While some choose to see failure as a calamity that must ruin them, others cheerfully consider it as a necessity in their quest for success.

People who make the best of failure are often those who don't consider failure an option in life. Whatever the circumstances may be, they know that they have no other choice but to succeed. Nothing can hold such people down or make them settle for a life of failure or mediocrity. To them, setbacks, disappointments, frustrations, oppositions and negative comments are nothing but catalysts to further reinforce their passion to succeed. The reason is simple: They have so shaped their mentality to see nothing else but success.

Let me refer to the life of Thomas Edison again. Between 1904 and 1914, he had spent a great deal of time and money trying to develop a number of devices. Sadly, on December 9, 1914, a huge explosion erupted in his factory and, within minutes, most of his works and equipment had been engulfed in the inferno. As the fire raged on, Edison's 24-year old son, Charles became absorbed in sorrow for his father. According to him, "My heart ached for him. He was 67 - no longer a young man - and everything was going up in flames." Interestingly, however, Edison's mentality was totally different. When he saw the ruins the next morning, he declared: "There is great value in disaster. All our mistakes are burned up. Thank God we can start anew." Unsurprisingly, about a year after, Edison had gone ahead to recover his losses and his company became even stronger.

It Hurts, I Know...

When I failed my nursing board exam twice, it was a devastating experience. I had been looking forward to passing and applying for a better job. Still, I did not let the failure end my career. I did not allow that failure to determine my future. I was determined to succeed, no matter what.

With this mindset, I reassessed my learning skills. I also reviewed the time that spent at home to take care of my newborn and other commitments that filled my day. I took refresher courses, planned my activities, and spent more time in the library to study harder than before. My focus was on the personal goal I made for my professional career.

When I sat for the nursing boards examination for the third time, I was successful with a passing score. Today, if I didn't tell anyone I had failed in the past, no one will know, because I have succeeded in many other things since that time. My life was not held back. I was resilient.

With the mentality of achieving success, you will readily know that the fact that you failed one time doesn't mean you will fail again. And even if you do, you would never see yourself as a failure, but see the experience as part of the necessary learning curve of your life. With each seeming setback, you are more determined to try again until you put failure to shame. As one writer has noted, there is usually a difference between what happens when a man says to himself, "I have failed three times", and what happens when he says, "I am a failure." Your mind is powerful and turning negative thoughts into positive thoughts is paramount.

Even the Bible says, "Though the righteous fall seven times, they rise again" (Proverbs 24:16, NIV). The logic is simple. Every true child of God knows that he or she possesses the DNA of the Almighty – a DNA that is naturally designed for success. It is inherently opposed to failure and limitation. So, what seems like failure to others, is, to you, simply a stepping stone to greatness. "And we know that all things work together for good to those who love God, to those who are the called according to His purpose." (Romans 8:28).

Settle it in your mind today that you are not made for failure. You don't belong in the valley of defeat or underachievement; you belong on the mountaintop of success and excellence. You are meant to succeed and be great in life; you are meant to be above and not beneath. You are meant to be part of the history-makers and record-breakers. You belong among those who cannot neither be restricted nor frustrated by failure!

Yes, Setback Happens!

Of course, the fact that you are destined for success doesn't automatically give you immunity against challenges. Indeed, the fact that you belong to the top is enough reason for you to pass through the refining and toughening furnace of failure.

Ryan Holiday, in his book, "The Obstacle Is the Way: The Timeless Art of Turning Trials into Triumph", says, "To do great things, we need to be able to endure tragedy and setbacks. We've got to love what we do and all that it entails, good and bad. We have to learn to find joy in every single thing that happens."

His observation is true. Challenges are an inevitable part of life. People with extraordinary destinies are especially prone to extraordinary challenges. It is a training process. The great men and women in history and the successful ones we still hear about today had their seasons of challenges. There are some that, when you hear of their stories, you would wonder how they ever managed to achieve anything meaningful in life.

The reality is that these are people who are resilient and will not give in or give up. The military men and women that you see today with many emblems of honor have equally gone through series of testing, exercising, intense labor, and hard work. Those skills prepared them to stand against any attack of the enemy, to stand still and fight to win. Be assured therefore that your challenges are no different.

The question now is, are you where you really wish to be in life? Are you enjoying every moment? Are there dreams, visions, and aspirations you are looking forward to? Whatever the case may be, you must never stop challenging yourself to do something bigger and better.

Think of Abraham Lincoln. Despite his catalogue of failures, he never stopped challenging himself to be better. He failed at many levels. He failed at war, he failed as a businessman, he failed as a lawyer, he failed at the early stage of his political career, but he did not give up because he knew that those temporary setbacks were part of what he must endure on his path to success. He knew that those challenges were to prepare him for the great responsibility embedded in his ultimate destiny. And truly, when Abraham Lincoln's moment arrived, he became the president of the United States of America – and one of the most remarkable for that matter. If he had given up, we wouldn't be talking about him today. He pressed on through all the challenges and made history.

The saying is true that what doesn't kill you makes you stronger. Besides, there is nothing so new or so outrageous under the sun. Whatever may have happened to you, whatever you may be going through, others have gone through same or even worse and emerged victorious. So, don't get so overwhelmed by your inadequacies or become so devastated by your challenges that you think your situation is hopeless or peculiar.

More importantly, you have this unfailing assurance that God will never allow you to go through circumstances that He hasn't given you sufficient grace to overcome. 1 Corinthians 10:13 says, "No temptation has overtaken you except such as is common to man; but God is faithful, who will not allow you to be tempted beyond what you are able, but with the temptation will also make the way of escape, that you may be able to bear it."

So, rest assured that you're in good hands. You're stronger than you think you are. If you can maintain the mindset of a champion amidst your challenges, everything will eventually turn around for your good. Your season of dryness will soon be over. It is simply a test of time and faith. Everything has a start date and an expiration date. That problem and challenge is about to expire and the testimony in it will be evident.

CHAPTER 3

YOU OWN YOUR POWER

3

YOU OWN YOUR POWER

Believe in yourself, and the rest will fall into place. Have faith in your own abilities, work hard, and there is nothing you cannot accomplish.

—Brad Henry

One of the ways of conquering thoughts of failure is to focus on what you have, not on what you're yet to possess. It is to appreciate who you really are, not who your critics think you are. It is to think of who is for you, not who is against you. In essence, it is to look away from your seeming inadequacies and focus instead on your blessings. And, yes, if you can think deeply and look closely enough, you would realize that there is indeed so much to keep you going, until your dreams and expectations come to full manifestation.

So, what areas of strength should you be focusing on?

You Have God On Your Side

I read somewhere of how young William Wilberforce was discouraged one night in the early 1790s after another defeat in his 10 year battle against the slave trade in England. Tired and frustrated, he opened his Bible and began to leaf through it. Just then, a small piece of paper fell out and fluttered to the floor. It was a letter that John Wesley had written to him shortly before his death.

Wilberforce read the letter again: "Unless the divine power has raised you up... I see not how you can go through your glorious enterprise in opposing that (abominable practice of slave trade), which is the scandal of religion, of England, and of human nature. Unless God has raised you up for this very thing, you will be worn out by the opposition of men and devils. But if God be for you, who can be against you? Are all of them together stronger than God? Oh, be not weary of well-doing. Go on in the name of God, and in the power of His might."

Of course, Wilberforce was renewed and he went on to succeed in his vision to see to the abolition of slavery in England.

Ask yourself the same scriptural question that Wesley asked Wilberforce: If God is for you, who or what can be against you? What challenge can you not overcome? What mountain can you not surmount? What opposition can you not subdue?

The Bible says in Daniel 11:32b, "the people who know their God shall be strong, and carry out great exploits." Do you know that you serve a God whose thoughts concerning you are continually thoughts of peace and not of evil (Jeremiah 29:11)? Do you know you serve a God whose primary desire for you is to prosper in every area of your life? (3 John 2). Do you know that you have a God who is able to do exceedingly, abundantly above all you can ask or think? (Ephesians 3: 20). Do you know that your God is the Almighty and with Him is no impossibility? (Jeremiah 32:27). No wonder the Psalmist says, "God has spoken once, twice I have heard this: That power belongs to God" (Psalm 62:11).

If you can fathom the magnitude of the God you serve and the high opinion He has of you, you will stop belittling yourself and paying attention to the negative opinions of people about you. Indeed, you will stop feeling intimidated by challenges and limitations. As the Scripture says in 1 John 4:4, "You are of God, little children, and have overcome them, because He who is in you is greater than he who is in the world."

The One who has got your back is the omnipotent and omniscient God. He is the one who can make something out of nothing; who can turn a mistake to a miracle; who can make a celebrity out of a nonentity.

> *"(As it is written, "I have made you a father of many nations")…God, who gives life to the dead and calls those things which do not exist as though they did"* (Romans 4:17).

Don't allow depression and dejection to pull you back from achieving what God has purposed for your life. God knows you even before you were formed in your mother's womb and He purposed you to reflect His image, glory and majesty. Regardless of the difficulties and limitations all around you, He is able to bring to pass all that He has programmed for your destiny. Your God is sufficient in all things and He will supply all your needs according to His riches in glory (Philippians 4:19).

The Potential for Greatness Lies in You

As a child of God, you have the seed of greatness in you. No circumstance can take this away. No degree of setback can destroy it. If only you knew what lies within you. If only you knew the extent of power and authority that is upon you, you would never look down on yourself or think less of yourself. And once you are so sure of yourself, when you have confidence and boldness that there is nothing stopping you, you will go out there and fulfill your purpose and reach your full potential.

I'm sure you must have heard the story of the eaglet that found himself among chickens. He would walk and peck the ground because he just didn't know that the power to fly lay within him and his wings. Oftentimes he would look up and see other eagles flying so high, but he simply considered himself to have been destined to live among chickens. He continued to go with the flow. But a day came that he decided to challenge the status quo (and I pray you begin to do so from now). He decided to try and fly like the eagles. He spread his wings, flapped it and prodded himself. Lo and behold, he was able to fly and join other eagles in the air.

That eaglet could have chosen to forever remain among the chickens and continue to peck the floor. But a day came – just as you're reading this book now – that he decided that enough was enough. He was no longer going to continue to underrate and undermine himself. And that decision brought a transforming reawakening to his destiny.

Indeed, the only limitation upon your destiny is that which you impose upon yourself. In reality, you were created to be a super achiever. So, what is stopping you from manifesting that which is within you? What is holding you back? What association clouds your identity?

Consider Gideon, who had always seen himself as a

worthless person because of his inferior background; yet God told him, "The Lord is with you, you mighty man of valor... Go in this might of yours, and you shall save Israel from the hand of the Midianites" (Judges 6:12-14). What about the Israelites who saw themselves as mere "grasshoppers", whereas even their enemies knew that the glory of God was mighty upon them and that no power could conquer them. What an irony!

There is an inner power in you that is desperately yearning for your activation. Unless you activate this potential within you, you may wander through life and never fulfill purpose and destiny. Today, I challenge you to re-examine yourself and re-evaluate your life. I challenge you to dare the big dreams, to pursue the big goals and vision and I can assure you that you will reach it in no time.

There is nothing to be afraid of except fear in itself. Fear is a torment and a weapon to hold you in captivity and to rob you of the fulfilled life that you've been destined to have. God has equipped you with all you need to succeed in life. God has made available all the resources that will take you from where you are right now, to where you are destined to be. The ultimate choice, however, lies with you. You can choose to remain a local champion, or dare to dream big and become an international champion. Don't settle for the less.

You are a Major Stakeholder in Your Destiny

Your destiny is not in the hands of some invisible forces that you cannot control. Sure, you might not have had any say on how or where you began your life but you do have a lot of influence on how you end it. You may not be able to do much about your past, but there is so much you can do to shape your future.

Let me show you something very interesting about the story of Esau and Jacob. We know that Jacob schemed and received the blessing of his brother, Esau. But then, when Esau pleaded with Isaac, his father, for just one blessing, Isaac told him something remarkable:

> *"Indeed I have made him your master…and you shall serve your brother; and it shall come to pass, when you become restless, that you shall break his yoke from your neck" (Genesis 27:37-40).*

Isn't this reassuring? "When you become restless, that you shall break his yoke from your neck." This means that the ultimate decision to break yourself free from every force that seeks to limit you rests with you. If you so decide, you can break free from every shackling experience that you've had, every hurtful comment you've heard, and make something memorable out of your life. This is exactly why George Bernard

Shaw, the Irish playwright, wrote: "People are always blaming their circumstances for what they are. I don't believe in circumstances. The people who get on in this world are the people who get up and look for the circumstances they want, and if they can't find them, make them."

The point is, much of what becomes of your life depends on you, not on your experiences or your environment. You have to decide the type of life you want to live. It does not matter what has been said of you. It does not matter the negative prophecies and pronouncements that have been uttered against you. If you could understand that you have the power to turn things around, that you have the ability to re-write your destiny, and you are willing to work hard and pay the price, then you will reverse every negativity; you will turn around every curse.

If you read the story of Jacob and Esau further in Genesis 33, after many years of exile and separation, when the two finally met again, Esau had become a great and wealthy man himself, so much that he had no reason to depend on his brother for anything. In fact, when Jacob tried to give him some of his possessions to make amends for past wrongs, Esau's reply to him was unequivocal:

"I have enough, my brother; keep what you have for yourself." (verse 9).

What does this tell you? The decision is yours - whether to settle for less and go with the flow, like a dead fish, or to challenge yourself and take giant steps to living a free, fulfilled, and accomplished life. Whatever you choose is exactly what you will have.

I recall how I challenged myself that, no matter what, I must continue my education until I achieve my master's degree. In between nursing school, I was co-pastoring with my husband, raising my kids and working full time. But because my mind was made up, I continued to work on my goals and dreams, and before I knew it, I had completed dual master's degrees: Master of Science in Nursing and Master of Business Administration.

Of course, it was difficult but I knew it was a sacrifice I had to make to get what I wanted. Many who had seen me juggling my various commitments and said I was daring the impossible, later came around to celebrate my achievements. Also, seeing that I had become the first in my family to earn a master's degree, my younger ones were motivated to continue their education and achieved success. Many of my friends and colleagues have been motivated by my achievement and tenacity and have gone back to school to get a higher degree.

Whatever you choose to settle for in life is your decision. Don't let anyone tell you that it can never happen or that you're meant to be a mere spectator in life. Success and greatness have no boundaries. They do not discriminate based on your color, gender or race; it all depends on your decision and determination. Greatness is not a respecter of person, gender, race or ethnicity.

When Barack Obama became the 44th president of the United States, he made history as the first African-American president. Even though no black person had ever occupied that position, Obama did not let that fact debar him from taking up the challenge. Despite the criticisms, mockery and antagonism that he faced, he was vigorous throughout his electioneering campaign. He did not accept failure as an option. He did not give up on himself; he did not allow the color of his skin or his background to hold him back. He worked tirelessly, aiming high for the White House. And, as you know, his efforts were rewarded. He broke record and became the first African-American president.

You Have Succeeded Before

Come to think of it – no matter how bad things are presently, or even how unfair you think life has been to you, your entire life couldn't have been all doom and gloom. You must have had some moments of success and achievement in your life - high school graduation, college graduation, raising a successful family, receiving recommendations, recognitions and awards, leading small groups, or implementing projects. If you have achieved any of these, then you have succeeded at one thing. And this is something to rejoice about because success can be replicated and repeated over and over again.

The same skills you used to succeed at one thing can be duplicated to achieve success at another. The same energy and strength you channeled towards one accomplishment can be used again. The same tenacity, the same discipline used in the time past can be used over again. This was the strategy that David deployed to conquer Goliath. This was a formidable giant that had intimidated the Israelites for 40 days and no one had been able to challenge.

But when David came to the battlefield, he remembered how God had helped him to conquer a lion and a bear and he believed that the same God would help him defeat the bragging giant. "And Saul said to David, "You are not able to go against this Philistine to fight with him; for you are a youth, and he a man of war from his youth." But David said to Saul, "Your servant used to keep his father's sheep, and when a lion or a bear came and took a lamb out of the flock, I went out after it and struck it, and delivered the lamb from its mouth; and when it arose against me, I caught it by its beard, and struck and killed it. Your servant has killed both lion and bear; and this uncircumcised Philistine will be like one of them, seeing he has defied the armies of the living God." Moreover David said, "The Lord, who delivered me from the paw of the lion and from the paw of the bear, He will deliver me from the hand of this Philistine" (1 Samuel 17:33-37).

And sure, with this high level of confidence and enthusiasm, he successfully brought down the enemy in record time. Regardless of the "Goliath" that may be threatening your peace, joy and progress in life, all you need do is recall your past victories and you would soon be dancing over the enemy. Build on the things you have accomplished in the past. If God has helped you in the past, He will not forsake you at this time.

Even if you think you have never experienced success before, you can learn from those who have succeeded, against all odds, to became great men and women in history. You can learn from them and start to make history. Read about successful people, listen to their stories and you will know that success and achieving greatness are possible.

CHAPTER 4

SUCCESS IS CLOSER THAN YOU THINK

4

SUCCESS IS CLOSER THAN YOU THINK

"Most great people have attained their greatest success just one step beyond their greatest failure."

– Napoleon Hill

If anyone had told Bette Nesmith that she was going to become a famous inventor and multi-millionaire within a few years, she probably would have dismissed it as a joke. One certain thing about her though was that she was a diligent worker and dogged optimist. And as the Bible says in Proverbs 22:29, "Do you see a man [or woman] who excels in his work? He will stand before kings; He will not stand before unknown men" – Bette's resilience was soon to pave way for greatness for her.

Bette was a secretary at the Texas Bank and Trust in Dallas. She did a lot of typing for the bank on her electric typewriter. Naturally, she sometimes made mistakes in her typing, which proved so difficult to correct. She soon became bothered about how best to correct the mistakes she made. Having had some art experience, she knew that many artists simply painted over their errors. She decided to adopt the same approach. So she prepared a white fluid to paint over her typing errors. When she tried the mixture, it worked perfectly! Soon after, other secretaries began to use her invention, which she called "Mistake Out".

Seeing the commercial prospects of the product, Bette attempted to sell the idea to marketing agencies and various companies, but they all turned her down. To them, the invention was simply not commercially viable. But Bette wasn't disturbed. Instead, she converted her kitchen into her first manufacturing facility and she started selling the product on her own. As the product's popularity began to soar, companies that had initially refused to buy into Bette's vision began to question their decision and were soon making offers to her. She eventually sold the enterprise to Gillette in 1979 at a whopping $47.5 million!

What does this tell you, reader? In the quest for success and breakthrough in life, quitters don't win and winners don't quit. If Bette had given up on her invention, based on the opinions of the companies she initially tried to market it to, we wouldn't be reading about her success story today. So, don't give up too soon. You may have labored hard and tried again and again, but I urge you to persist a little bit more, until your breakthrough becomes a reality.

You're Pregnant with Success

The struggles that often precede the fulfillment of a dream and the joys that come after can be compared with what happens in pregnancy and childbirth. When a woman is about to give birth, particularly through the natural process, the pain will be so intense; but sooner or later, as she pushes one more time, the baby will be delivered.

This is why doctors and other healthcare professionals will not allow the mother to give up, especially when the baby is crowning, because if she does, she may lose the baby. These professionals can see what the woman cannot see (just as God knows the great breakthrough that is about to happen to you). This is why they often give all the support and encouragement for the woman to push just one more time, just one more time, and then she will feel the relief as she hears the cry of the baby. The overwhelming joy that instantly floods her soul will almost make her forget the agony she had been through.

I remember when I was in labor with my first child. He took me 12 hours of labor. My doctor almost gave up on me and they wanted to prepare me for a Cesarean section, but one of my nurses kept encouraging me with words like, "You are almost there; we can see the head of the baby, if you can just push one more time". With the support that was available, I was able to push through and delivered my first bouncing baby boy. Though I still remember what I went through, it is a lasting joy each day to see the resultant blessing. He is almost 10 years old now.

The Scripture is true: "Weeping may endure for a night, but joy comes in the morning"(Psalms 30:5). It's only few hours from the night till the day breaks. Surely, your joy will come. Of course, it may sometimes appear as if you're laboring in vain. It may seem like you're just wasting your time with the efforts you're making, but I tell you that all your toiling and tears are being noticed in heaven – and all will work towards the realization of your breakthrough. It was Jacob Riis, Danish-American reformer, that once rightly said, "When nothing seems to help, I go and look at a stonecutter hammering away at his rock perhaps a hundred times without as much as a crack showing in it. Yet at the hundred and first blow it will split in two, and I know it was not that blow that did it, but all that had gone before."

Sometimes, what seems to you like a delay in fulfillment of your expectations may just be a matter of timing. As the Bible says, "To everything there is a season, a time for every purpose under heaven" (Ecclesiastes 3:1). When a seed is planted in the ground, it does not bear fruit the same day. It goes through the necessary process of germination. It will require a lot of nurturing which includes watering and trimming, and then the time of harvest will come. To put it simply, there is a time lapse between planting and harvesting. So, keep on nurturing the seed of greatness in you. Keep on working towards the fulfillment of your God-given dream. At the appointed time, your destiny will burst forth like the brightness of the dawn – to the delightful surprise of all, including yourself. God's word confirms this: "Those who sow in tears shall reap in joy. He who continually goes forth weeping, bearing seed for sowing, shall doubtless come again with rejoicing, bringing his sheaves with him" (Psalm 26:5-6).

Also, note that in farming, the time of harvest differs, depending on the seed. With some seeds, you can reap the harvest in weeks or months; but with others, it may be years. If you give up on the plant before it's time to bear fruit, you will lose the harvest and someone else will reap the fruits of what they have not sown. So, you have to persist in tending to the plant of your destiny, until the fruit is ripe and ready for harvest. Galatians 6:9 says, "And let us not be weary in well doing: for in due season we shall reap, if we faint not."

Don't Stop Until You Attain

This is a great success secret. When God started the works of creation, He did not rest until He had completed the work on the seventh day. When Isaac was to have a well in the valley of Gerar, he did not stop digging – despite the cruel vexations of the enemy – until he achieved the goal. Genesis 26:19-22 says, "Isaac's servants dug in the valley, and found a well of running water there. But the herdsmen of Gerar quarreled with Isaac's herdsmen, saying, "The water is ours." So he called the name of the well Esek, because they quarreled with him. Then they dug another well, and they quarreled over that one also. So he called its name Sitnah. And he moved from there and dug another well, and they did not quarrel over it. So he called its name Rehoboth, because he said, "For now the Lord has made room for us, and we shall be fruitful in the land."

Your own Rehoboth too is coming, but you must not give up till you get there. In the meantime, continue to build on the momentum. As it happened with Isaac and his servants, the enemy will always try to frustrate, weaken and discourage you. He will use people, he will use circumstances - all with the aim of making you lose focus. But if you can continue with the same momentum, if you can continue to push through, if you can stay strong against all odds and continue to persist and work consistently, in due time, your breakthrough will emerge.

This reminds me of the story of Hannah in the Bible. As we're told in I Samuel 1, her rival, Peninah, did everything to make her life miserable. She continually mocked her and hurt her feelings because she was yet to have a child. Yet, Hannah never stopped going to Shiloh, the house of God. There, she would pray and not faint, trusting and believing God for a miracle. One of such visitations to Shiloh, as she was praying, the prophet of God noticed her, and affirmed her prayer and faith. Soon after, she gave birth to a son, Samuel, who became the greatest prophet in his time. If you refuse to give up, your long awaited miracle will manifest and become a reality.

There is also the story of the widow woman told by Jesus in Luke 18. Each time the woman went to the judge of the city to ask him to avenge her of her enemies, the judge paid no attention to her. But the woman persisted, until, one day, the judge was forced to grant her desire. According to him, "Though I do not fear God nor regard man, yet because this widow troubles me I will avenge her, lest by her continual coming she weary me." (verses 4-5)

The judge had no other choice than to grant the request of the widow. But what if she had given up just a day before her request was granted? She certainly would have missed her miracle. Every obstacle on your way is to make you stronger and tougher for what lies ahead of you. I always say that the word "NO" does not mean denial; it means next opportunity. Don't give up when there seems to be obstacles on your path. If you quit at the edge of success, if you faint and give up, you would have just wasted your time and resources and you will remain or be in a worse shape than when you started.

You're Almost There

The reward of consistence and persistence is breakthrough. When the going is very tough, and you feel you can't take it anymore, just keep on, because success is closer than you think. Let me tell you, the more the pressure, the closer you are to success than you can think or imagine. Some people quit when they were almost there, which means that they had only wasted their labor and time. Just as soon as they left, someone else stepped in, worked a little and reaped the reward.

I remember watching Super Bowl 51 - the match

between Atlanta Falcons and the New England Patriots. The game was so extraordinary that a reporter for The Atlantic later described it as "The Super Bowl That Felt Like Destiny" – and I quite agree with him. At the beginning of the game, the Falcons were doing very well. They had a very strong defense and the players seemed extremely ready to win. It was a good start for them. By half time, it was 28-3 in the favor of the Falcons. Surprisingly, however, by the end of regulation time, the Patriots had leveled up the score: 28-28!

I could not believe such a comeback from the Patriots. Indeed, no team had ever dug out of such a large hole in the history of the Super Bowl. The crowning climax was that by the end of the extra time, it was still the Patriots that emerged champions.

Interestingly, while the Patriots were still trailing far behind the Falcons, one of our friends watching the game with us had stated that the Patriots might stage a comeback because it was untypical of them to succumb to defeat. And they did just that!

Certainly, the Patriots could have given up. Mere looking at the scoreboard should have killed their enthusiasm. They had many reasons not to put in the extra effort to win. But they chose to persist, to work harder, to remain focused – and they ended up winning the game and going home with the trophy. This further confirms one established truth about life. It is not about how you started or when you started, but how you finish.

So, how are you seeing yourself in the game of life? Are you feeling you will never make it? Are you thinking everything is against you and nothing is in your favor? I encourage you to push through. I encourage you to work a little harder. I encourage you to strengthen your inner man and continue to pursue until you overcome. People do not celebrate those who give in to failure but those who, after failing, get up and work harder to reach their goal!

CHAPTER 5

PREPARING FOR YOUR BIG BREAK

5

PREPARING FOR YOUR BIG BREAK

"Success is the sum of small efforts - repeated day in and day out."

—Robert Collier

Now that you are fully convinced that you're destined for a glorious future, regardless of your present circumstances, what do you do while waiting for the manifestation of this great expectation? What should preoccupy your time and mind as a potential achiever and record-breaker?

1. Be grateful for today. Have an attitude of gratitude. However unpleasant things may seem around you, there is always something to be thankful for. The little you think God has done, express your appreciation. It is He who has brought you this far. The fact that you are still alive is, in itself, a good reason to be grateful.

As the Bible says, "a living dog is better than a dead lion" (Ecclesiastes 9:4).

Many people would give so much to have what you have today and to be where you are at this point in your life. All you are and all you can ever hope to be is by the grace of God (1 Corinthians 15:10). If you can acknowledge God, appreciate Him for what He has done, for what He is doing at present, and for what He will continue to do, you will continue to see Him in action.

There is an adage in my place in western Nigeria that when a child is grateful for the things he received yesterday, he will surely receive more today. Zig Ziglar affirms this truth when he said, "Gratitude is the healthiest of all human emotions. The more you express gratitude for what you have, the more likely you will have even more to express gratitude for."

Take time to assess yourself in this regard: Have you been insensitive to God's goodness? Do you take His blessings for granted? If so, then things must change, if you want God to accelerate your breakthrough. Praise Him like never before. Worship Him for who He is and what He is able to do, and soon, your mouth will be daily filled with new songs of praise.

There is this saying that if you have tried prayer and you are yet to have what you ask, then try praise. The more you praise God, the more He opens the heavens over your life.

2. Make positive decrees over your life. The power of life and death is in your tongue. And God has declared that when you decree a thing, it shall be established unto you (Job 22:28, KJV). When you make positive confessions over your life and your situation, things will turn around for your good. So, avoid confessing negativity. Avoid cursing or berating yourself.

Declare positivity every day. For example, instead of using your mouth to confirm the negative things that Satan tries to bring to your mind, simply reverse it instead and make declarations like: I am stress-free. I am the best at what I do. People want to do business with me. I am the head and not the tail. I am above and not below. The hands of God are upon me. I receive favor everywhere I go. I am preferred above my colleagues. Doors are opening for me. Whatever I ask, I receive. Whatever door I knock, it is opened. Lights are shinning unto me in pleasant places. I am blessed. Everything I touch is blessed. Afflictions shall not rise again in my life. The Egyptians I see today, I will see them no more. I can do all things through Christ who strengthens me. I am a winner, not a loser. I am a victor, not a victim.

Don't accept failure and rejection. It is not your portion. No matter what the enemy is saying to your hearing, no matter what is happening around you, resist the temptation to entertain fear and negative confessions. This was the error of the Israelites and the major reason multitudes of them perished on their way to their God-ordained destiny. After they had made a number of negative confessions concerning themselves, God simply told them: "Just as you have spoken in My hearing, so I will do to you" (Numbers 14:28). Since you know then that God listens to every declaration you make concerning yourself to perform it, you must make it a habit to say only what you wish to see.

And should someone make a negative prophecy or pronouncement concerning any area of your life, reject it instantly. Few years ago, my son was having issues with his blood count. The doctor gave all kinds of medications but none seemed to be able to boost his blood level. Consequently, the doctor came to the conclusion that he might be suffering from leukemia and wanted to send him for more tests. Instantly, my husband and I rejected the confession and the disease. We took our boy home, prayed for him, continued with the current medication, gave him communion every day and constantly declared restoration and good health upon him. Few weeks later, when we went for another test, the blood count had recovered!

Let no man or situation confuse you. The plan of God for you is a better and fulfilled life. "For I know the thoughts that I think toward you, says the LORD, thoughts of peace and not of evil, to give you a future and a hope" (Jeremiah 29:11). Daily and boldly declare the promises of God for your life, and you will see your situation aligning with your proclamations and declarations.

3. Maintain a cheerful composure. No matter what the situation is, no matter the feeling inside, always reflect the joy of the Lord on your outside. Allow the light of God to shine through you. Don't allow any situation to change your demeanor. Don't lose your cool because of what is going on around you. Don't allow the enemy to tamper with your mind.

The Bible says that "If you faint in the day of adversity, your strength is small" (Proverbs 24:10). If people around you or those who come in contact with you always have to know whenever things seem not to be going well for you (through your attitude), that will portray a sign of immaturity or faithlessness.

Besides – and this is very important - you never can tell when you will meet your angel, your destiny-helper, someone who will take you to the next level that you've been yearning for; someone who will be instrumental to your success and greatness.

Do you know that with just one connection, your life can be changed forever? But if you always keep a sad face, always frowning or snarling at people, you may unwittingly chase your destiny helpers away.

The world is not a perfect place. Not everyone wants what you want. Not everyone is happy with you chasing after your dreams. But, despite all the negativity, despite all the hatred and reproach, keep the right attitude. Know that when the enemy is after you, his goal is to distract you from your vision, so that you can instead focus your energy on negativity and profitless labor.

Therefore, you must, in your own best interest, keep the right attitude. It is said that two wrongs do not make a right. You are a light and you must maintain your identity, no matter the plan and plot of the enemy against you.

Do not let someone else rain on your parade; do not let someone hinder you from what lies ahead of you. Forgive quickly and move on. Your happiness and peace of mind are totally dependent upon you. Maintaining a positive attitude does not necessarily mean that you are pleased with all that's going on around you; it just shows that you have chosen to take control over them rather than letting them control you.

Remember the story of Esther in the Bible. When she heard of the plot of Haman against the Jewish people, she maintained a calm posture and attitude. She did not lose her temper or lash out in anger. She sought the face of God for guidance on what to do. And God gave her specific instructions. When she did accordingly, Haman's plot against Mordecai and the Jews backfired on him.

If Esther had pursued the matter with anger and decided to handled it her own way, she wouldn't have made it alive and the Jews in the land would have been completely wiped off. When you keep the right attitude, you will be able to harness all your energy and efforts toward productivity. You will be able to think straight and act accordingly. You will work out your plans in wisdom and achieve that which you have proposed.

What about Hannah, whose story we considered earlier? Her case was even more peculiar (and very instructive) because the temptation to lose her emotions and react negatively did not only come from Peninah, her rival, but also from the high priest himself, who she would have expected to be more understanding and sympathetic. As she knelt down in Shiloh, pouring her heart out to God in supplication, all Eli could perceive in her actions were the antics of a drunken woman. And he addressed her accordingly:

"How long will you be drunk? Put your wine away from you!" (1 Samuel 2:14).

This was probably a divinely-ordained test for Hannah. And, thank God, she passed! Rather than expressing disappointment and displeasure at the unwarranted rebuke, she simply explained her true condition to the high priest with remarkable calmness and reverence. "No, my lord," she said. "I am a woman of sorrowful spirit. I have drunk neither wine nor intoxicating drink, but have poured out my soul before the Lord. Do not consider your maidservant a wicked woman, for out of the abundance of my complaint and grief I have spoken until now" (verses 15-16).

That did it for the high priest. He was so touched by her attitude that he placed a seal of blessing on her petition. And from then on, her story changed forever.

What if Hannah had allowed herself to "snap" and lashed out at Eli? You and I can easily guess what the result would have been. God is not the author of confusion; He is the God of order. Having a grip over your emotions is part of the fruit of the Spirit. It is also a leadership skill and trait. If you cannot control your emotions, how can you expect to be placed in a position of responsibility? If you are prone to temper tantrums or emotional outbursts, how can you be trusted with great success and wealth?

It is true that your gifts can sometimes take you to the top, but only your character can keep you there. If people know you to be emotionally weak and unstable, they will sooner or later relegate you to a position where you just work in silo. Keeping the right attitude is a sign of maturity. You don't respond to every negative talk or speech. You maintain your integrity, personality, and dignity. Keep your head high in all situations!

CHAPTER 6

REACH OUT FOR GREATER HEIGHTS

6

REACH OUT FOR GREATER HEIGHTS

"The heights by great men reached and kept were not attained by sudden flight, but they, while their companions slept, were toiling upward in the night"

—Henry Wadsworth Longfellow

One key principle you must imbibe, in addition to all we have considered in the previous chapters, is the undying thirst for self-improvement. This is a major preparatory step to greatness. It is one thing to hope for the best, but it is quite another to make yourself fit and available for the opportunity for greatness when it comes.

If you recall the story of Wilma Rudolph in the first chapter, you will observe that between the time of her first Olympics outing and the one for which she is best remembered, she devoted herself to a rigorous regime of self-development in order to attain her dream. To quote her again, "I ran and ran and ran every day, and I acquired this sense of determination, this sense of spirit that I would never, never give up, no matter what else happened."

As we saw earlier, too, before David could conquer Goliath, he had trained himself to confront and conquer wild beasts. He had developed himself to withstand opposition and demonstrate the potentials in him. And so, when the opportunity came for him to move to the next level in his life through the threat posed by Goliath, he rose to the occasion and was fittingly rewarded. Also before Joseph could become a Prime Minister in Egypt, he had learned to be a good administrator in Portiphar's house and in prison – as well as being able to network with others who could be of help to him, as his interaction with Pharaoh's butler demonstrates.

There have been stories of people who were said to be eagerly praying and waiting for a breakthrough in their lives but when the opportunity finally came by way of a job or contract that could totally transform their lives, they were found unprepared, either during the selection process or within a short time of taking up the offer. So, apart all the other principles of success you have learned so far, also take note of the following:

Sharpen your Skills, Seek Knowledge

Ignorance is never an excuse for failing in life. Indeed, when you're ignorant in areas where you are supposed to be knowledgeable, it can cost you a lot - time, resources, years, and even your very life. The reason many people have remained in the valley of defeat and deprivation is their lack of knowledge. God Himself said, "My people are destroyed for lack of knowledge" (Hosea 4:6).

If you don't know, you will be robbed of your opportunities, rights and blessings. If you lack adequate and up-to-date information on areas of life that concern you, you will remain stagnated in life. This requires deliberate efforts on your part to stay abreast of current issues, trends and developments, especially in your areas of interest. The information you know in times past, may never be relevant again to current realities. Things are changing rapidly and you need to adapt where necessary.

Gone are the days when information is only shared through the conventional media. These days, people use e-mails, smartphones, and all forms of networking platforms, such as Facebook, Instagram, LinkedIn, Periscope, Skype, just to name a few. You can attend school online and at anywhere. So, these days, you can't complain of limitation caused by geographical location. You can be in the United States and do business with people in United Kingdom or in China.

What this requires is that you consciously seek information and sharpen your skills to expand your opportunities. Don't limit yourself to one idea or area. Don't rely just on your educational degree. Seek for certification and advanced courses to better improve yourself. Seek to continually get better at whatever you are doing. Make yourself an expert, an indispensable expert!

The story of Jacob provides us with a good example of how ignorance can subject one to a life of hardship and needless waste of precious years of one's life. Genesis 29: 18-27 says,

> *"Now Jacob loved Rachel; so he said, "I will serve you seven years for Rachel your younger daughter." And Laban said, "It is better that I give her to you than that I should give her to another man. Stay with me." So Jacob served seven years for Rachel, and they seemed only a few days to him because of the love he had for her. Then Jacob said to Laban, "Give me my wife, for my days are fulfilled, that I may go in to her." And Laban gathered together all the men of the place and made a feast. Now it came to pass in the evening, that he took Leah his daughter and brought her to Jacob; and he went in to her. And Laban gave his maid Zilpah to his daughter Leah as a maid.*

So it came to pass in the morning, that behold, it was Leah. And he said to Laban, "What is this you have done to me? Was it not for Rachel that I served you? Why then have you deceived me?" And Laban said, "It must not be done so in our country, to give the younger before the firstborn. Fulfill her week, and we will give you this one also for the service which you will serve with me still another seven years."

While there is no denying that Laban himself was a man of deceit, the problem here was that Jacob had been so consumed by his love for Rachel that he had volunteered to serve Laban for seven years to get her. Assuming he had properly inquired about the law of the land, he would have known that it was unacceptable to give the younger sister out in marriage, until the older one had been married. But because he did not inquire, he had wasted seven good years before he was told that he could not marry Rachel. He had to serve for another seven years, making it a total of fourteen years, just to marry the one he loved.

This situation is all too common today. We have had people who spent several years in school, struggling to study a course they were never suited for. There have been people who entered into deals, agreements, relationships and partnerships that have continued to prevent them from making progress in life – all because they were not properly enlightened.

If you have found yourself in such a situation, I pray that God will grant you favor and deliver you.

Connect with Experts and Mentors

It was Sir Isaac Newton, the revolutionary scientist, who once said, "If I have seen further than others, it is by standing upon the shoulders of giants." This is an indisputable reality of life. You need to learn from others. Whatever is it that you are going through; or whatever it is that you want to accomplish, know that someone has been there before.

Someone has already achieved that which you are pursuing; someone has already attained that status you are aiming at, and someone has already encountered victory in that battle you are faced with. So, reach out to people and learn from them. "He who walks with wise men will be wise" – so says the Holy Scripture (Proverbs 13:19).

Sometimes, we try to do things on our own. We depend on our knowledge to carry us as we journey to the next level of our lives. But this often leads to avoidable errors, pitfalls and missed opportunities. The truth is that there are certain times and specific situations that require adequate learning and mentoring. For instance, why do we go to school? Why do we learn a trade? The reason is because we want to acquire skills and knowledge that can guide us to make the right decisions and fulfill our dreams in life.

Having a right mentor and teacher will speed up your success in life. Having a mentor or a coach will save you from many headaches and many sleepless nights, as you tap from their wealth of experience to forge your own path in life. Note again – you're not choosing a mentor or learning from others because you're expected to copy their principles and beliefs but so that you can receive lessons and guidance from them on how you can decide to shape your life. It is for this same purpose that I mentioned much earlier that you can read the biographies of people who have succeeded in your field of interest or those who have successfully turned challenges to testimonies in their lives. This way, you can learn about principles of success in career, business, marriage and so on.

Now, how do you choose a suitable mentor or guide? First, consider the Holy Spirit. The Bible says that one of the chief functions of the Holy Spirit is to guide us into all truth. Don't underestimate the impact that the Holy Spirit can make in your life. If you seek God at the earlier stage of your projects, be sure He will guide you. If you let God and his Spirit take the front seat, you will make less mistakes, you will have the strength and grace to accomplish those goals and achieve greatness in life. Proverbs 3:5-6 says, "Trust in the Lord with all your heart, And lean not on your own understanding; In all your ways acknowledge Him, And He shall direct your paths."

So, note it again that your first and best mentor is the Spirit of God. Other coaches include people who have the Spirit of God, who are trustworthy, respectable and approachable. Also, depending on the seasons and stages of your life, you may have to change mentors. There is nothing wrong with this. The key thing is to know what you want and who you can trust to help you get it. Above all, you must be teachable, coachable and willing to be mentored.

Do Not Compromise

Never forget this in all you're seeking to achieve. No matter the pressure, no matter what you are faced with, do not compromise. Do not tarnish your image with things that will come back to haunt and hurt you. Do not cut corners. There is time for everything. At the appointed time, God will lift you up.

To have lasting success in life, you have to stay away from practices that will adversely affect you. You have to avoid behaviors that will lead to damaging reviews and references. Note that bad news spread faster and what people hear of you cannot be unheard.

Trying to seek help from the devil or his agents; or giving yourself up to sin so you could acquire something will be detrimental to you and your future. Consider the story of Joseph again. His brothers had sold him to slavery, so that he would not realize his dreams. While in slavery, he found himself in Potiphar's house. His master loved him so much that he made him to be in charge of all he had. As time went on, Satan raised Potiphar's wife against him and she began to pester him to have an affair with her. Joseph could have fallen victim to the trap of the enemy by committing immorality and sinning against God. And, perhaps, he might have even been able to conceal it from anyone else; but he would have ended up mortgaging his destiny because he wouldn't have gone to the prison - which had been divinely prepared as the avenue through which he would become the first Prime Minister of Egypt.

Thank God that Joseph maintained his integrity. Rather than compromising with his master's wife, he simply replied:

> "Look, my master does not know what is with me in the house, and he has committed all that he has to my hand. There is no one greater in this house than I, nor has he kept back anything from me but you, because you are his wife. How then can I do this great wickedness, and sin against God?" (Genesis 39:8-9).

Joseph, indeed, took a wise decision. There is a proverb in my place that says that a lie may last for a while, but the truth will eventually catch up with it. Whatever is done in darkness will come to the light; it's just a matter of time. We cannot help God to fulfill His promise – whatever He says He will do, He will surely do it.

Some people had committed atrocities to get ahead in life, believing they would never be found out, only to realize that they had been deceiving themselves. Galatians 6:7 says, "Do not be deceived, God is not mocked; for whatever a man sows, that he will also reap." No sinner will go unpunished. Every act comes with its own consequences. There are many who should have had a glorious destiny, with a beautiful legacy, only for them to end up their lives in shame and regrets.

This reminds me of the story of a famous actor and celebrity in the United States. Everybody loved and respected him. He had become like a father-figure to many African-Americans. However, in his old age, buried secrets - atrocities that he had committed more than two decades earlier - began to come to light. Many women came out to recount how he molested and raped them. In his old age, this globally-acclaimed celebrity lost his place and became a spectacle of ridicule.

What legacy do you want to leave behind you? The temporary joy and pleasure of doing the wrong things cannot be compared to the shame and dishonor that will come later on in life. And by that time, bad deeds cannot be undone. People will not be able to reason with you to understand your motives. You will lose close friends and acquaintances; you will be alone and depressed. This is why you must think carefully about the steps you take today, because the shape of your tomorrow depends on them.

CHAPTER 7

FOCUS ON THE REWARDS

7

FOCUS ON THE REWARDS

"To succeed in life you need not only initiative, but also finishiative."

—Zaida Jones Blaine

Florence Chadwick was not new to long-distance swimming. She had, in fact, been the first woman to swim the English Channel in both directions. So, when on July 4, 1952, she attempted to swim from Catalina Island to the California coast, it came as no surprise. This time, however, she had much more to contend with. To start with, the weather was challenging because the ocean was ice-cold, and the fog was so thick she could barely see the support boats that followed her. The tides and current were against her. And, to make matters worse, sharks were in the area.

Still, against all odds, Florence decided to swim. Hour

after hour, she swam on. Sadly, after almost sixteen hours of swimming, she asked her support crew to take her out of the water. She couldn't continue any longer. The reason was not because of the many hurdles she had to contend with; the problem was that, because of the fog, she could not see the coastline, where she was supposed to end her race. Ironically, the coastline was just less than a mile away. When reporters asked her later why she couldn't continue, she replied: "If I could have seen land I know I could have made it."

This is perhaps the best secret of most people who have surmounted challenges and recorded great achievements throughout history. Ability to keep the rewards of their labors in focus. Going through challenges and difficulties is not naturally comfortable; and it is normal for one to be tempted to give in to discouragement. But once the final rewards become the object of focus, rather than the temporary discomforts, there will always be motivation to continue till the end.

Jesus Christ is our perfect example in this. Hebrews 12:2 says, "Looking unto Jesus, the author and finisher of our faith, who for the joy that was set before Him endured the cross, despising the shame, and has sat down at the right hand of the throne of God." Jesus, in dying for mankind, endured cruel betrayal, accusations, beatings, humiliations, mockeries and excruciating agonies. It was not easy, but one thing kept Him through it all: the joy that awaited Him – the joy of fulfilling the will of the Father and redeeming mankind from the captivity of Satan.

We read earlier too about Jacob who did not mind serving Laban for seven years, just to be able to marry Rachel. The most interesting part of it is the manner in which he handled the period of his servitude. Genesis 29:20 says, "So Jacob served seven years for Rachel, and they seemed only a few days to him because of the love he had for her."

What kept Jacob going and reduced years of labor to days of fun in his mind was the reward awaiting him – beautiful Rachel. Even when, after seven years, his father denied him Rachel, citing cultural reasons, Jacob was still willing to serve for another seven years!

What kept Stephen strong while being stoned to death? His eyes were fixed on the waiting arms of Jesus (Acts 7:55-56). Why was Paul not afraid when it was time for him to be brutally killed? He said it himself: "For I am already being poured out as a drink offering, and the time of my departure is at hand. I have fought the good fight, I have finished the race, I have kept the faith. Finally, there is laid up for me the crown of righteousness, which the Lord, the righteous Judge, will give to me on that Day…" (2 Timothy 4:6-8).

If you can learn to be more concerned about the

potential rewards of your struggles, rather than the struggles themselves, you will develop the strength and courage to win. I pray that the Lord will give you the grace and strength to finish every noble project or endeavor you have embarked upon.

Are you half-way through school? Are you working extra hard on that job or business? Success is around the corner, victory awaits you. Imagine how your life will be transformed, if you achieve your goals. Imagine how your success story will affect so many lives and how your achievement will be recorded and be used over and over to encourage others to pursue their dreams. These are thoughts that should occupy your mind.

When David conquered Goliath, the whole city celebrated him. They sang and danced to appreciate him. His fame travelled abroad. The same will be for you when you achieve your goal. When you reach the heights that people considered impossible. When you break records and live a fulfilled life.

Moreover, when you become an achiever, you will be noticed. People that matter will want to associate themselves with you. People will want to learn from you, so they could achieve their goals as well. Why do people attend programs organized by notable leaders like John Maxwell and Les Brown? It's because these people have sacrificed a lot, they have pushed through challenges, and succeeded. What about you? How do you want to make history?

Another blessing that comes with fulfilling your dreams is that people will take you seriously wherever you go. Imagine how your status will change and how many lives will be impacted if you don't give up. One movie that has impacted me so much is "Hidden Figures" – which tells the story of three women who made significant impact in space. They fought through discrimination and rejection, they worked extra hard, they persevered, they never gave up. If they had given up, the world wouldn't be telling their story today. Now their lives have impacted other people; they have opened doors of opportunities for the less privileged, for people of color and for women.

It's Your Turn

You too can be celebrated. If you can fight for your dreams till the end, there will be no limit to your success and greatness in life. This is your season of harvest. You have labored for so long and soon, it will be time to reap your reward.

A laborer is entitled to his wages. You have been in that situation for so long and you are coming out shortly. Your trial and tribulation are coming to an end. There is time for everything - time to go through stuff and time to come out, time to face challenges and time to celebrate, time to fight and time to win. Your season of celebration is here.

As I said earlier, every problem has an expiration date. God is a rewarder of those who diligently seek Him and He will not withhold any good thing from you. The enemy has lost the battle over your destiny; there is nothing anyone can do about it.

When the brothers of Joseph sold him into slavery, their intention was to prevent him from amounting to anything in life. But God turned it around for his good. All that they meant for evil, God turned it around in Joseph's favor. It became a process for his dreams to materialize. Though there were times when it would have seemed that he had been forgotten, but his day of accomplishment and celebration eventually came. He was elevated and his brothers eventually bowed to him. He had the last laugh — just as you will have the last laugh over every challenge and opposition. That's how God works!

This is your appointed time, friend. Wipe your tears and tap into your God-appointed season of breakthrough. Break every yoke that has been limiting you. Break into singing and dancing. Begin to give God the glory because your promotion is here. Your glory can no longer be covered. I see you rising and shinning. Every veil covering your glory has been lifted; every curse is broken, and every limitation and restriction has been lifted. I celebrate God for your life. YOU ARE UNSTOPPABLE!

ABOUT VICTORIA SHOWUNMI

Victoria Showunmi is the co-founder of Destinystar Ministries International and ministers alongside her husband, Pastor Gbenga Showunmi. Her faith in God is heavily influenced by her parents who are senior pastors in The Redeemed Christian Church of God.

She is a practical and down to earth teacher of the word and her passion to empower women to succeed in every sphere of life is unwavering. She is the President of Victoria Achiever's Club, and Founder of Women Empowerment Forum, a community of women with the mission to Empower, Enrich and Encourage other women.

Victoria is a Registered Nurse who holds MSN and MBA. She is a champion for the broken and hopeless. She is the mother of three wonderful children: Toluwani, Oluwatobi, and Temitayo.

NOTE

NOTE

NOTE

NOTE

NOTE

www.ingramcontent.com/pod-product-compliance
Lightning Source LLC
Chambersburg PA
CBHW031602040426
42452CB00006B/382